THE DETAILED INTERIOR

The Detailed Interior

DECORATING UP CLOSE
WITH CULLMAN & KRAVIS

ELISSA CULLMAN
AND TRACEY PRUZAN

THE MONACELLI PRESS

CONTENTS

INTRODUCTION 6

FRENCH FORTIES ON THE PARK 8

GEORGIAN ELEGANCE 26

UP COUNTRY MAUI 52

LUMINOUS LUXURY 72

RUSTIC REDUX 84

ASIAN FUSION 106

PALM BEACH PUNCH 122

FIFTH AVENUE FINESSE 148

HIGH STYLE IN A HIGH RISE 166

A MIDCENTURY MOUNTAIN RETREAT 180

MODERN TRADITIONAL 190

CELEBRATING AMERICANA 206

VENETIAN VISION 234

FRENCH FLAIR 248

PROJECT CREDITS 270

ACKNOWLEDGMENTS 271

INTRODUCTION

When we published our first book, *Decorating Master Class*, we set out to demystify the decorating process by explaining the inspiration and the logic behind our design approach. Still, there are so many choices involved in decorating a room that we decided to write a new book—one that would focus less on the big picture and more on the specifics. In this book, we turn our attention to the details..

Mies van der Rohe's famous dictum "God is in the details" has always inspired us. Mies recognized that the fine points of design are just as critical to aesthetic success as the overall conception. We, too, are passionate about the details. We like to say that inspired rooms are more than just pretty—they have an underlying logic and layering of information. Whether it's the inclusion of a motif that relates to geographical location, a connection we make between a client's beloved collection and a fabric scheme, or simply an emotion that the room itself evokes, the details create a more wholly integrated environment—rich with meaning, full of sparkle and life.

We have given a great deal of thought to how we could both educate and delight you with the presentation of this material. To this end, we have traveled around the country and taken extra care to include all new photography of our work, including plenty of up-close photographs to provide an intimate view. We wrote captions to specifically address the design decisions these images reveal, such as nuances of style, shape, texture, and especially the connectivity of our ideas.

In the tour that follows—which reveals some of our favorite projects never before published—we hope to inspire and guide you on your own decorating journey. Whether the design vocabulary is high style or folk art, traditional or contemporary, disciplined or whimsical, these interiors all celebrate our passion for details and the great pleasure we take in articulating these ideas for our clients, for ourselves, and now for you.

FRENCH FORTIES ON THE PARK

H IGH ABOVE NEW YORK'S CENTRAL PARK IN a historic hotel sits this airy apartment with unobstructed views from every window. Such extraordinary real estate demands an exceptional approach. Inspired by French Art Deco design and by mood-defining interiors of movies from the 1940s, this pied-à-terre was transformed into a wholly modern retreat that highlights the owner's passion for vintage and contemporary photography from masters such as Georges Brassai and Diane Arbus to exciting younger artists such as Nan Goldin and Vik Muniz.

The original floor plan was respected, but each room was studied, reproportioned, and repurposed to accommodate the client's life in the city. Three bedrooms soon turned into one master bedroom, a sitting room/guest room, and two separate studies with closets and baths attached. An unexpected extra space was converted to a gym.

A neutral palette complements the ever-changing collection of photographs. Cream and celadon colored materials range from luxurious suede to shagreen to imported horsehair. Walls are covered in leather, grass cloth, and cashmere or painted in high-gloss finishes like faux-crocodile Venetian plaster. Most of the furniture pieces are antiques by prominent Art Deco makers including E.-J. Ruhlmann, Jules Leleu, and Jacques Adnet. Where period pieces were not available to support modern functions—such as a cabinet to house a flat screen TV—we worked with local artisans to create period-inspired originals. Silk curtains throughout are beaded, studded, hand-painted, or embroidered, adding sumptuous layers of glamour to the overall design.

The entry sets the stage with a crema marfil and onyx floor encircled by brass inlay. A gilded dome ceiling and clean white Venetian plaster walls let the photographs shine. The oak and gilt-bronze console table by Jacques Adnet holds a Barbara Hepworth sculpture from 1959. Above it hangs an Art Moderne mirror enhanced by an etched band following the shape of the frame. The ledge in the gallery allows for easy rotation of photographs, some of which also hang on the walls and lean on the floor.

PREVIOUS PAGES: A classic living room furniture plan of comfortable sofas, side tables with lamps, and a glass-topped coffee table focuses attention on the photographs, including two by Vik Muniz. ABOVE: The cabinet, based on a design by De Coene Frères, was custom made to allow extra depth for the TV lift. The Jacques Lipchitz sculpture is secured to the top. RIGHT: An early-twentieth-century Swedish commode, Jules Leleu sycamore chairs upholstered in unglazed crocodile, and a Nan Goldin photograph peacefully coexist. Even the Royal Copenhagen stoneware with bronze lids feels at home in this eclectic mix.

ABOVE, LEFT: The top of the dining table was found at the Marché aux Puces. Made of brass and hammered copper, it was originally the bottom of a chandelier. ABOVE, RIGHT: Couture embroidery from Lesage of metallic beads and silk threads adds opulent detail to curtains and pillows. RIGHT: The intimate dining area takes advantage of the magnificent view of Central Park. A hand-tufted wool and silk rug incorporates a monumental Greek key motif.

RIGHT: Inspired by the designs of Charles Ruhlmann and Jules Leleu, respectively, the desk and chair are newly made on a small scale to fit the compact study. High-gloss walls with inset leather panels add bespoke detail. Glass-paneled pocket doors connect with the living room. ABOVE: The powder room details—metallic-thread grass cloth, a custom vanity with molding faux gilded to look like metal—relate to the study.

LEFT: A leather and bronze-detailed desk is in the style of André Arbus. Faux snakeskin upholstered chairs, a shagreen desk lamp, and walls glazed bronze and varnished to a high gloss add layers of texture. ABOVE, LEFT: Saddle-stitched cashmere pillows and a hand-embroidered blanket complement the feminine feeling of vintage fashion photographs. ABOVE, RIGHT: A 1940s sycamore and parchment vanity and stool are from France. Bronze lozenge nail heads are set three inches from the curtain panel edges so that this couture detail does not get lost in the folds.

LEFT: Sumptuous celadon cashmere envelops the master bedroom walls and bed. A hand-painted stencil runs along the edges of the silk curtains. Limestone-topped side tables made by a Brooklyn craftsman pay homage to the straw marquetry work of Jean-Michel Frank while vintage Murano glass bedside lamps add a translucent shimmer. ABOVE: Upholstered chairs in bedrooms are often a little smaller and more tailored than those in a living room. The pillow is embroidered with raffia.

The guest bedroom is set up as a sitting room with a Murphy bed that folds out from the opposite wall. The carefully composed geometry of the decoration extends from the carpet design and the pillow embroidery to the nesting tables and the Art Moderne gilt-bronze geometric lamps. Pony-skin ottomans add extra seating. The walls are painted in faux crocodile Venetian plaster with a pearlescent wax to add sheen. The trim was glazed and varnished to match.

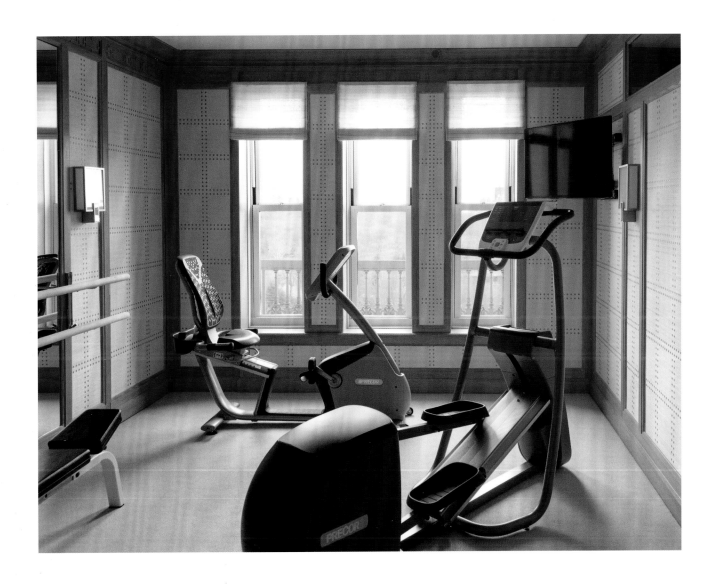

LEFT: A set of six photographs by Jiang Yiming hides the Murphy bed, but the bronze pull subtly gives it away. The Art Deco side chairs are upholstered in cream leather. ABOVE: Instead of another guest room or a family room, the owners opted for a gym that boasts spectacular views. Fully detailed with cerused-oak trim and studded grass-cloth walls, the space fits in seamlessly with the aesthetic of the apartment.

GEORGIAN ELEGANCE

THIS GEORGIAN-STYLE HOUSE ON ONE HUNDRED acres of rolling farmland in New Jersey is newly built, but it feels as if it has been there for 150 years. A layered, strongly geometric architectural plan creates well-proportioned rooms of generous size, all of which maximize views through the house, and out and across the site.

Volumes and shapes of rooms change throughout, creating natural circulation patterns and helping guests intuitively differentiate public and private spaces. Regal thirteen-foot-high ceilings, complex plaster moldings, and antique leaded-glass overdoors give the house a sense of age, while the three dining rooms—one formal, one intimate, plus a breakfast room—accommodate the demands of modern life. Parts of the house feel palatial and grand, but as a whole, the traditionally conceived spaces radiate livability and warmth.

Decoration, of course, had to be commensurate with the scale and complexity of the architecture, which meant furniture and art had to be of the very highest quality. Every gesture counts, and was carefully considered. Modern art plays an especially important role here, bringing energy and spark to this grand house. Not only does the art of the present enliven the past—the antiques and decorative objects from the past add history and character to ths newly built home.

In the entrance hall, the Edwin Lutyens–inspired floor pattern made from Porto Beige and Lagos Azul limestone mitigates the scale and adds drama, movement, and tension. A bronze Tony Cragg sculpture, although modern, fits well under the traditional banister—its twists and turns echo those of the floor and stair.

ABOVE: A large house demands a grand entrance. This elliptical reception room sets a formal tone with its domed ceiling and Ionic columns. RIGHT: In this "opposites attract" composition, a colorful painting by Frank Stella from the 1960s hangs above a George III settee covered in ribbed silk. Side tables are often very hard to find, especially ones that are just the the right height, width, and material. This one was newly made in Paris.

ABOVE: An oversize console in the entry is an appropriate scale for the grand space. A Kenneth Noland painting is hung opposite to be reflected in the mirror. RIGHT: A commanding nineteenth-century red-ground Sultanabad rug in the living room sets the palette for the entire house. OVERLEAF: Two full seating areas fit comfortably within the generous proportions of the living room. The Regency center table subtly divides the room.

ABOVE: Red and gold tones dominate the living room, making the hit of sky blue provided by a Robert Motherwell painting pop and feel like one of the windows facing it on the opposite wall.
RIGHT: Large rooms require many objects to help them feel fully furnished; pairs help to structure a room so that relationships between pieces can be easily understood. Gilded rococo lines on a pair of Chippendale mirrors flanking the fireplace, for example, contrast with the modern art without visual overstimulation.

ABOVE: Detail of the raised relief of the Berlin pottery vase on the center table in the living room.
RIGHT: The octagonal sitting room, though less formal than the living room, is distinctly
elegant. Cinnabar paint on the walls flows directly from the ground color of the rug in the
adjacent living room. A pair of Japanese Meiji period bronze trumpet vases converted to lamps
flanks the sofa; the coffee table features a specimen marble top and a carved mahogany base.

ABOVE AND RIGHT: The blue palette in the library is a peaceful respite from the saturated red and gold living room across the hall. Blue-and-white Chinese porcelain on the shelves stands out against the rich brown cabinetwork and echoes the palette of the rug.

ABOVE: Paired consoles gilded in white and yellow gold flank the opening
between the hall and the dining room; the matched mirrors feature
both plate and convex glass. RIGHT: Chandeliers are the forgotten
step-children of contemporary decorating; the right piece adds a glow
to a room that drenches an entire space in light. This five-foot-tall ormolu-
and-cut-glass Empire chandelier from 1815 features a metal crown made of
feathers that adds visual weight without compromising radiance.
This commanding piece draws the eye to a fluted ceiling medallion and
the corresponding form echoed in the drape of the curtain heading.

ABOVE: In the china hall, stenciling is used instead of carpet to add warmth and pattern.
RIGHT: The small dining room is shaped like a bell jar, with a double-height, gilded dome ceiling. Shimmering gold accents on the embossed leather seats, in the art, on the glazed walls, and on the iridescent curtain fabric create a tone-on-tone effect.

ABOVE: The semicircular end of the kitchen overlooks a cutting garden. Because the architecture, with its undulating plaster ceiling moldings and complex cabinetry design, is already layered, understated simple roman shades are all the embellishment the windows require. RIGHT: The breakfast room has an elongated, silvered-bronze chandelier and full-length curtains that quietly match the roman shades in the connecting kitchen. The restrained decoration allows the view to take center stage.

ABOVE: An antique textile purchased in London inspired the design of a custom-made rug for the master bedroom. The whorls of the dense, hand-tufted wool serve as a counterpoint to the elaborate plasterwork details on the ceiling. RIGHT: Saturated yellow Venetian plaster walls highlight the refined millwork. A strong color, like vibrant yellow, is critical for supporting the architecture of such a robustly detailed room.

ABOVE, CLOCKWISE FROM TOP LEFT: A detail of an eighteenth-century Danish neoclassical mirror frame; gilding on the églomisé panels in the dressing room; a pair of Ming dynasty court figures on the coffee table; the curvilinear pattern of the master bedroom rug.
RIGHT: A magnificent pair of Chinese Export beaker vases on the mantel.

LEFT: Master bath details include a gilded dome ceiling, slab onyx floors, and gilt-bronze lights and hardware. ABOVE: In her dressing room, deep sills provide an opportunity for window seats with silk cushions and café curtains.

UP COUNTRY MAUI

A FEW YEARS AGO, WE HAD THE PLEASURE OF a phone call from Oprah Winfrey. After seeing Ellie's Connecticut house on the cover of *Architectural Digest*, she decided that Cullman & Kravis would be the right firm to decorate her new home in Hawaii.

After decorating the main house, we turned our attention to the four cottages tucked into her magnificent property, once a well-known bed and breakfast and now a working horse ranch. Oprah wanted to respect the original architecture yet transform the complex into a retreat for friends, family, and colleagues to gather and mingle, to read and cook, to collaborate and create. Most important, this was to be a quiet haven for hiking, walking, biking, swimming, or riding. There are no cars or roads, only one television, and plenty of books—most of which Oprah herself has read.

Two major themes guided the design direction. One was that the house should be filled with classic upholstered furniture, antiques, and fabrics that would all reflect a distinctly American point of view rather than a tropical one. The other was that figures of dogs and horses, two of Oprah's passions, fashioned from wood, iron, tin, and stone would be used as sculpture and decoration to weave a connective stylistic motif throughout the complex.

The architecture was reworked and updated, but the traditional Hawaiian farmhouse style characteristic of many historic homes on Maui and Honolulu, which Oprah loves, has been preserved. The American country aesthetic that dominates the interiors embodies the best elements of a new recipe for year-round gracious living.

RIGHT: A limestone floor, trellised walls, French doors, and a sky-lit ceiling bring the outdoors into the dining room. Six square tables allow for maximum flexibility as they can be pushed together or separated to accommodate any size group. A Swedish gesso chandelier from the 1940s hangs in the center. A nineteenth-century rooster weather vane and an early-twentieth-century peacock garden ornament are sculptural focal points in this sunny room. OVERLEAF: The colorful and airy living room was designed around the palette and pattern of the hand-woven Elizabeth Eakins rug.

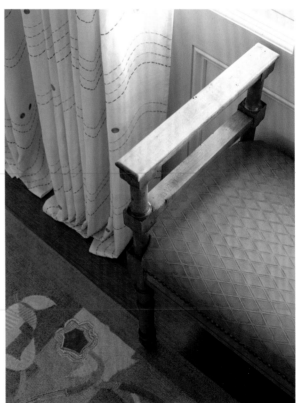

ABOVE, CLOCKWISE FROM TOP LEFT: One of a pair of eighteenth-century Italian polychrome putti; carved oak chest and a faux-marble mirror frame above; Charles X bench with embossed leather beside linen curtains embroidered in a wavy design by Ranjit Ahuja in Bombay; pine mantel, c. 1800, from the Hudson Valley. RIGHT: An iconic Edward Hopper painting evokes the character of the ranch. A sturdy camphorwood trunk is used as a coffee table.

LEFT: In the library, shades of green look soothing surrounded by light-colored pine paneling; both colors combine in the plaid fabric on the sofa. Tufted leather Swedish club chairs, a bobbin-turned canterbury, and a brass-studded teak trunk from Zanzibar add interest. Between the windows is a nineteenth-century Noah's Ark, once a child's toy and now considered sculpture by folk art collectors. ABOVE: A photograph from the series Oprah commissioned of the foliage and animals on the property.

ABOVE: The breakfast table in the kitchen is at counter height to encourage lingering over morning coffee and having fun at cooking lessons. Celebrating the tradition of farming and ranching, Oprah likes her guests to participate, helping with the cooking rather than simply waiting to be served. RIGHT: The fresh green shade of Costa Esmerelda stone counters, repeated in the fabrics and accessories, enhances the domestic ambience of the chef-style kitchen. Shelves on the ends of the island relieve the mass and add a country farm table personality.

ABOVE AND RIGHT: This guest bedroom features a broad tray ceiling with coffers and V-groove boards, a private balcony, and a four-poster bed. The pastel palette of sea-foam green and periwinkle blue is enriched by antiques like a midcentury gilt chandelier and a walnut table with iron stretchers, both from Spain, and faux-bamboo chairs from France. The embroidered linen curtains are unlined and hang from metal poles and rings, letting in lots of Hawaiian sunlight.

RIGHT: In the living room of one of the cottages, the sisal and linen diamond-patterned rug suggests a relaxed feeling, and the palette is filtered and softened compared to the main house, but the furnishings and art are no less humbly elegant. Sky blue glazed walls set off distinctive details like a pair of zinc star finials and a grass-cloth panel in the coffee table top.

ABOVE, LEFT: The nineteenth-century chandelier and tiger maple satinwood chairs in the dining area were found in Philadelphia. ABOVE, RIGHT: A nineteenth-century painted pull toy.

ABOVE: Each of the eleven bedrooms is designed as if for a family member with its own palette of natural materials, antique furniture and objects, art, and books. Signature antiques like an eighteenth-century French writing table, alabaster lamps, a bleached-cherry commode, and a white spool bed all add tremendous character and warmth. RIGHT: Contrast fabric inset on the headboard and bed skirt, tape binding on the Gustavian oval-backed desk chair, and a pair of nineteenth-century Swedish bedside tables elevate this bedroom from country cottage to country couture.

LEFT: In the living room of another cottage, an exposed-timber ceiling with V-groove boards and locally sourced lava stone on the fireplace surround is more rustic than the main house.
ABOVE: Every effort was made to communicate Oprah's desire for a warm and welcoming feeling in every space. From honey-beige glazed walls to a friendly dog and a red-painted horse, all the details in this entry feel lighthearted and easy-going.

LEFT: Cool shades of hyacinth and lavender create a serene space conducive to creative thinking.
ABOVE: In the cottages, while still evoking Americana, the design vocabulary was broadened
to include country pieces from Europe. The painted bench and the gray-blue commode are both
late-nineteenth-century Swedish, and the painted toy horse is English and antique.

LUMINOUS LUXURY

T HIS PIED-À-TERRE IN ONE OF FIFTH AVENUE'S most distinctive buildings features eleven-foot-high ceilings, north and west exposures, and a hexagonal living room. For this project, a subdued yet impressive architectural vocabulary was established, including new floors, doors, and moldings, to highlight the distinctive space. At the same time, the primary design goal was to create a sympathetic background for an art collection that includes works by Robert Motherwell, Gerhard Richter, and Damien Hirst. Since much of the art is very vibrant and somewhat arresting—the client's first purchase was a shocking pink Anne Truit that hangs in the living room—the overall color scheme is based on luminous but muted tones.

The owners requested luxurious fabrics and finishes; because they only use the apartment occasionally, the decoration could include delicate materials. Consequently, fine hand-tufted wool rugs, and pale velvet and woven silk upholstery fabrics abound. Details such as custom-embroidered curtain cuffs with jeweled accents in the living room, cashmere-upholstered walls in the library, and crosshatch Venetian stucco in the entry embody the refinement and articulation that defines this unique environment.

As a counterpoint to the modern art and the contemporary feeling of the textiles and paint finishes, the furnishings and lighting fixtures are traditional. Antiques are often gilded but never overwrought and instead radiate an appealing and welcoming ambience in keeping with the idea that this a second home for refreshing weekends in the city and for entertaining intimate groups of friends and family.

When the apartment was first purchased, the far wall was fully mirrored—clearly a departure from the original design intent. It is restored more in line with the period architecture, using a mantel from London inlaid with Bardiglio marble as a focal point. The palette and design of all rooms in a house should be based at least loosely around the living room rug; this subtly textured wool carpet, which was cut on site to fit the unusually shaped room, establishes a lightly hued palette and a preference for custom work of the highest quality, while its shaded grid pattern anchors the room and provides a design motif echoed by the curtain cuff embroidery.

 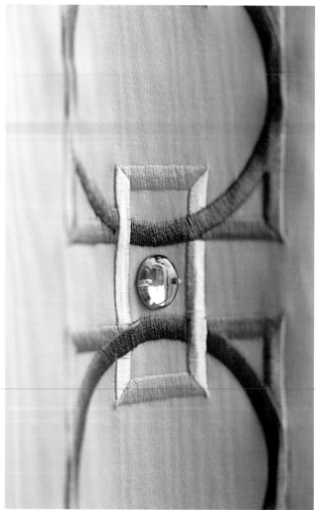

ABOVE, LEFT: An oval mirror repeats the geometry of the inlaid marble mantel and the arched doorway, while the frame's golden color contrasts with the stone's cool tone to create subtle contrast.
ABOVE, RIGHT: The contrast between metallics of various hues and round and square shapes continues in the decorative embroidery of the curtains. The mirrored bead adds a sophisticated wink of fun.
RIGHT AND OVERLEAF: Paintings with jolts of powerful color, like this one by Anne Truit, can be hung successfully in places other than on the white walls of a gallery or in an all-white loft. Muted gray and beige interiors, warmed up by antiques like an Austrian chandelier and by traditional upholstery forms like a skirted sofa, translate into an appropriately supportive domestic vocabulary for the display of modern art.

ABOVE: Inlaid ebony is all the decoration an entry hall floor needs. A strategically placed mirror reflects daylight from the living room, the library, and the kitchen into the space, helping it feel open and airy. RIGHT: Earthy metallic tones in a gilt-wood mirror frame, bronze lamp, and chestnut-colored stone on a bronze console with a custom Marron Cohiba stone top accentuate the hot colors of a painting by Jon Thompson, reflected in the mirror.

Libraries are often decorated in a more restful palette than other rooms. A soothing jade-colored chenille sofa, walls upholstered in celadon suede, and a striped carpet in muted shades of green and tan distinguish this space. The discreet tones set off a painting by Heimo Zobernig with its unusual surface of Swarovski stones embedded in acrylic binder. The unobtrusive but unique streamlined Art Deco chandelier is bronze.

ABOVE: Chair rails provide another dimension to wall surface treatment, and they also define the waistline of a room, much like a belt. RIGHT: Hand-carved cherry-wood Biedermeier side chairs in a golden honey tone complement the muted tones in the library. The reflectiveness of the glass, steel, and gilt-bronze round table by Maison Jansen adds crispness to a room otherwise characterized by plush materials.

RUSTIC REDUX

THIS WORKING RANCH, SET AMID 12,000 PRISTINE acres in Colorado, was conceived as a year-round retreat for a family concerned with environmental stewardship at a philosophical level, and, at a personal level, with comfort. The Western aesthetic of wide-open skies is clearly the point of departure for the architecture, but to render the almost overwhelming panorama of the exterior vistas relaxing for family and guests, the rooms and furniture are intimately scaled. The resulting design emphasizes grandeur, but still allows anyone to tromp through with mud on his shoes with no great consequence to the interior.

The structure, realized in timber and stone, instantly conveys solidity, whereas the subtle palette of the furnishings only reveals itself quietly, upon close examination. A broad range of brown and green tones in the principal rooms references the landscape in colors, including olive, oatmeal, sage, caramel, camouflage, and khaki. The clients requested smooth, soft, and sleek fabrics and carpets, so custom linens, cashmere upholstery fabrics, and handwoven wool rugs are abundant. As a whole, the house is characterized by pronounced simplicity overlaid with great richness.

In any mountain retreat, there is always the temptation and opportunity to employ a traditionally Western vocabulary, but here it was strategically redefined in unexpected ways. Instead of using rough-hewn furniture, for example, the rooms are filled with English and French pieces—bobbin turning and metal strap work render them sympathetic to rustic materials nearby. Nods to the house's location and purpose are indulged, however, with details like whip-stitched pillow and lampshade edges, embossed and woven leather, and hand-forged iron hardware.

Jean-Michel Frank style sofas and a newly woven rug anchor the living room, which is embellished with pieces of various origins and of disparate styles and finishes. A cowhide-upholstered Irish oak chair, for example, is the quintessential "personality chair." Antique wing chairs are upholstered in weathered leather to render them welcoming and to beckon guests to their cozy position next to the fireplace.

ABOVE: Jack Goldstein's dramatic portrait of a lightning storm amplifies the experience of the grand outdoors, which is seen from the living room windows. Corduroy sofa fabric and cashmere pillows hand-embroidered in wool sateen convey the tactile experience of the room. RIGHT: Custom ottomans with leather handles and exposed saddle stitching are conveniently stowed beneath a rustic farm table when not in use as extra seating.

TEEPEE SMOKE

Karl Bodmer's America

LEFT: To make the house feel cocoon-like in every season, heavier fabrics are interspersed with lighter ones. Jute-embroidered linen curtains and cashmere-embroidered sofa pillows look at home with traditional English bobbin benches recovered in woven leather and a new game table with a wrought-iron base. ABOVE, LEFT: The entry hall introduces the architectural vocabulary of stone and timber, including Colorado stone flooring, wall stones set with visible grout joints, and beams and lintels made of rough-hewn planks. ABOVE, RIGHT: In the entry, an antique antler console is paired with a new mirror framed in leather inset with nail heads.

ABOVE: Details give the kitchen a strong character in keeping with the rest of the house. The yellow tone was inspired by an early purchase—a collection of nineteenth-century yellow-ware bowls. Both the cleft-face Zimbabwean granite counters and the butcher block island are extra thick to indicate a rural setting, and the "Old Hickory" stools are a rustic classic. RIGHT: French *os de mouton* chairs, when upholstered in caramel leather and embellished with oversized nail heads, look at home in the wilderness. The overscale trestle base and plank top relate the dining table to the architecture and setting.

PREVIOUS PAGES: Natural wood and rough-hewn stone in the sitting room reflect an appreciation for traditional craftsmanship. Butternut-colored pine and a Colorado limestone hearth are offset by chamois-colored stucco walls and the laid-back tones of sage and terracotta. Antique augers and calipers have a sculptural quality. ABOVE AND RIGHT: Wooden pieces in a variety of forms engender a rustic atmosphere in the study. An Arts and Crafts walnut library table with an intricately carved edge and a trestle base, a side table with a freeform top and legs, and cabinetry that is hand stained in sage green and inset with hand-blown glass all contribute. A multicolored rug in a basket weave design adds vibrancy.

ABOVE, CLOCKWISE FROM TOP LEFT: A nineteenth-century German folk art cabinet with relief carving; Mike and Doug Starn snowflake prints adorn the wall above the bed, with linens embroidered in a custom design that evokes barbed wire; the freestanding oval tub is set up on a platform to take advantage of the view; a pair of antique mirrors keeps the bathroom from looking overly built in or too contemporary. RIGHT: An Art Populaire twig sofa from the late nineteenth century, a fur throw, Jaspe pitchers, and cashmere plaid fabric reinforce the sense of luxury.

PREVIOUS PAGES: The large barn connects to the main house, but the decoration has a different spirit with rough-hewn beams, lively weather vanes, and vibrant antique board games. LEFT: In the barn, unique Arts and Crafts chairs with wavy back splats surround a table with an industrial metal base. Stairs lead to a loft where a band plays for parties. ABOVE: Under the loft, old saddles were mounted as bar stools. The red wall brackets the red leather banquette at the other end of the room.

ABOVE, CLOCKWISE FROM TOP LEFT: Even the most refined details pay tribute to the location: the modern form of a Jean-Michel Frank style sofa is tempered with boldly scaled, lumberjack plaid wool; a large coffee table features a reclaimed top made from an antique, star-patterned floor; the built-in banquette has cheerful cherry leather upholstery; the ends of chair arms feature a long-horned steer motif. RIGHT: A pair of antler chairs upholstered in deerskin offer the perfect setting for a fireside chat.

LEFT: The guest cottage is set 150 yards away from the main house, but its details are equally considered. Art Deco–style chairs are upholstered with Moroccan rugs set into the leather upholstery, and burlap curtains feature decorative tape trim embellished with wooden buttons. ABOVE: Bunk beds with timber frames share space happily with an Italian eighteenth-century painted commode and a pair of chain-link lamps. The bed linens are embroidered with the ranch's brand in lieu of a monogram.

ASIAN FUSION

THIS FAMILY, WHO RETURNED TO NEW YORK after ten years in Tokyo, immediately connected with Ellie, who had also lived in Japan. Sharing a similar passion, she and the clients determined from the outset to incorporate Japanese screens, armor, Chinese porcelain, pottery, and the like into the design of this classic Stanford White townhouse of 1904.

The envelope of the interiors is traditional, with classic and high quality furniture from the nineteenth century, primarily English. Oriental carpets are used in the principal public rooms—a Persian Kirman in the living room and a Turkish Oushak in the dining room. When contemporary art was selected, it was critical that the work was sympathetic to the Asian point of view that the house embraces. Artists such as Helen Frankenthaler and Pat Steir were chosen, both of whom were inspired by the aesthetics and abstraction of the Far East.

The house also reflects the passion of the young family members living there. Consummate sports fans, they requested certain concessions—all furniture and fabrics are comfortable, durable, and conducive to watching sports or playing games from billiards to basketball. There is a television in every room—even the living room and dining room—so every minute of every precious game can be watched.

The result is a generous and elegant townhouse, a distinctive home that comfortably accommodates both an Asian inspired art collection and the active young family who lives there.

A complete set of armor from Japan's Edo period commands attention and serves as a strong vertical focal point in a large living room. Two small Japanese chests are used as coffee tables. An octagonal tilt-top side table made from amaranth and satinwood complements the lacquer and polychrome of the Asian artifacts. Antique Chinese embroidery fragments sewn onto new gold silk taffeta add distinction to throw pillows.

Symmetrical windows, French doors, and twelve-foot-high ceilings announce the living room as a formal space. A 50-inch-tall, cut-glass chandelier helps fill the enormous overhead area. Lavish silk curtains with hand-embroidered cuffs are mounted on oversized, gilded-mahogany hardware to contribute a feeling of strength. The center panel was mounted on a wooden, framed arch to draw particular attention to the shape of the window. An intricately patterned and richly colored antique Persian Kirman rug ties the color scheme together and helps to anchor the tall, vertical room.

ABOVE: The curtain, hand embroidered with an anthemion motif, is lined and interlined to protect the delicate silk fabric from the sun. RIGHT: The mate to this burled-walnut chest, one of a pair that flanks the living room fireplace, has been "surgically altered" to hold a flat-screen TV on a hydraulic lift. Ignoring the taboo on televisions in the living room activates the formal space.

ABOVE: This Japanned cabinet on a stand supports a lacquer basin filled with hand-blown glass buoys. A pair of oversized blanc de chine vases adds visual interest below. Like white linens or a fresh white shirt, white accessories can clarify a composition. RIGHT: A black lacquer coffee table, custom made in France, incorporates Japanese family crests and gilt-bronze.

LEFT: The texture of a Pat Steir painting and a painted pottery horse from the Northern Wei dynasty contrasts with the smooth white marble of an English mantel.
ABOVE: A boldly carved and gilded eighteenth-century Spanish mirror is a dramatic foil to the restrained lines of a nineteenth-century Swedish chest. Mirrors and paintings hung above chests or consoles should always be slightly narrower than the furniture below.

ABOVE: Aside from holidays and celebrations, dining rooms are often left dark and unused. In this case, the owner suggested that the dining room could double as a billiards room. The custom-made dining table is actually a pool table that drops at the press of a button to dining-table height. When topped with lightweight, interlocking wood panels and covered with a long tablecloth, it can seat twelve comfortably. The rosewood credenza houses a flat-screen TV on a hydraulic lift.
LEFT: The Regency center table doubles as a kids' table at large family gatherings.

Wood paneling is associated with luxury, but the dark background it creates can be oppressive. Here gold, crystal, and silver reflect flashes of light deep into the interior. Cinnabar on the tablecloth, decorative plates, and in the screen adds vibrancy. Small arrangements like these, composed of white hydrangeas, ranunculus, and apricot-colored orchids, are an ideal way to set a long table. A centerpiece of a reclining wooden Buddha on a bronze stand adds drama.

LEFT: An eclectic mix of decorative objects from around the world helps to situate predominantly Asian pieces within the townhouse's classical architecture. Three unglazed, Han dynasty, Sichuan pottery figures of musicians rest on the mantel in front of a mirror in a late-nineteenth-century American frame, and three Yoroi helmets from the eighteenth-century Edo period in Japan hover on the wood paneling, where their full shape can be appreciated. ABOVE, LEFT AND RIGHT: A set of seventeen green-glazed figures of musicians from sixteenth-century China are carefully stabilized to rise up on top of the sideboard's concealed television without toppling.

PALM BEACH PUNCH

WHEN THESE LONGSTANDING CLIENTS BOUGHT this landmarked house, designed by noted architect John Volk in 1931, its great bones had been obscured by a series of earlier renovations. Windows were covered or lost, wooden coffered ceilings were painted over, and the tropical feeling of sunshine and light was missing. Undaunted by the monumental task of modernizing the entire structure and restoring many of the original details, our client brought a contagious enthusiasm and exceptional vision to the project. The house is now injected with a tremendous sense of fun and a new point of view through the palette, the furniture, and the artwork.

The completed house is at once rustic and opulent. Typical Palm Beach materials like wrought iron, Spanish tiles, and pecky cypress are juxtaposed with sophisticated surfaces like lacquer, shagreen, and Venetian stucco walls studded with stones. Bedrooms in energetic shades of honeydew, mango, and turquoise and a family room glazed in rich hues of coral are emblematic of the southern location and of our client's great delight in decorating her new home.

The design mantra was "If you love it, it will work," and the result is a collection of eclectic and modern interiors. If our client agreed that a piece had a sense of humor—corkscrew-shaped bar stools or a parrot sculpture built with playing cards, for example—into the scheme it went. And in turn, the client brought so many exciting bits of whimsy and humor into the mix, notably a bright yellow sculpture that reads "YO" when seen from one side and "OY" when seen from the other, that the delightful result is a boundless feeling of freedom and joy in this gracious house in Palm Beach.

In the living room, a silk shag area rug, tailored upholstery, and stuccoed walls all in fresh shades of cream help organize seemingly unrelated items such as orange linen curtains, embroidered by Lesage with a border of bone beads and French knots in camel-colored parchment, and a pair of sinuous 1940s French rope twist tables. Leopard silk velvet on the Jansen chair adds a bold shot of pattern, while the colors of the flowers in the Bill Beckley photograph reflect the palette of the room.

Tall casement windows and the original pecky cypress cathedral ceiling emphasize the expansive ease of the room. A Royere design inspired the two-tiered chandelier with its sinuous iron structure. A vintage pair of Louis XVI-style caned chairs were stripped to their natural pine and upholstered in Fortuny cotton to support a sense of rustic opulence. On the far wall, nineteenth-century orientalist fruitwood and walnut tables flank the fireplace; a Theodore Stamos painting hangs over the mantel.

ABOVE, CLOCKWISE FROM TOP LEFT: One of a pair of sleek metal lamps with bronzed-metal drum shades; linen pillows embroidered with bone beads and ribbon chain stitch and trimmed with glass beads; custom-colored glass balls on metal wires are installed as a divider between the living room and loggia; brushed-steel and bronze chest with a black granite top below a Moroccan mother-of-pearl mirror frame. RIGHT: An acid green shagreen table with midcentury modern–inspired chairs upholstered in Fortuny cotton exemplifies the strong mix of objects and surfaces.

LEFT: In the loggia, cushions on the wicker furniture are hand painted in a custom stencil design similar to the glass screen. The coffee table has an oil-rubbed bronze base and a silver-leafed glass top. Flanking the sofa, twentieth-century brass, resin, and steel lamps rest on custom wooden tables with lacquer tops and a border of nail heads.
ABOVE: Coil-shaped stools are gilded, adding light and a little shimmer under the bar. The client's sense of humor is revealed in the YO sculpture by Deborah Kass.

ABOVE: Typical of many Palm Beach houses, faux rusticated stone in a running bond pattern on the foyer walls begins to blur the lines between interior and exterior, as does the original terracotta tile floor set with colorful cabochons. Mediterranean ceramic tiles in different patterns are set on the stair risers. A muscular iron baluster and a lacquered bench upholstered in Mongolian lamb soften the stone stairway, while a parrot made of playing cards welcomes every guest. LEFT: A Regency-style bone-veneer bench, found on a shopping trip to London, centers the entrance hall.

LEFT: A large-scale decorative plaster pattern brings texture to the dining room ceiling, which was designed without a chandelier to facilitate parties with more than one table. A six-panel cinnabar lacquer screen by the 1940s Parisian master Bernard Dunand adds a sculptural dimension to the walls. ABOVE: Details like textured metallic Venetian plaster walls, laser-cut felt curtains with raffia stitching, and an Italian console from the 1950s with carved faux-rope detail benefit from the relief of plain sisal carpet with leather binding. The Mel Bochner monoprint is a prized possession.

ABOVE: Venetian stucco powder room walls are stenciled with silver paint and inlaid with blue amazonite stones. The mirrored glass of the Art Deco vanity is etched in a twisting-knot design. RIGHT: Within the framework of traditional paneling, the library feels tropical with light-colored pecky cypress wood, a relaxed sectional sofa, and a seafaring palette of lagoon blue and lemon yellow. Dyed-blue raffia stitched in a wave design on the sofa pillows anchors the location. A Roman shade adds pattern without fuss.

ABOVE: The kitchen, always the hub of activity, opens to the pool through a wall of French doors. The large scale of the floor stencil balances the large repeat of the paisley chair fabric. RIGHT: Sun filters in and enlivens intense coral-glazed walls in the family room. A U-shaped sectional sofa is an ideal configuration in a family room because two can recline and four can sit. Coral polka-dot chair fabric is a fanciful interpretation of the animal-print motif found throughout the house.

PREVIOUS PAGES: The margarita green toile fabric on the walls inspired the master bedroom design. An array of luxurious materials includes a silk-and-wool carpet, white linen curtains with a vivid green cuff, and a gold leaf bed with an aqua mohair throw draped over the custom linens. Just the right scale, the lacquered chinoiserie and églomisé bedside cabinets were made in France about 1940. A gilt-metal and chrome seahorse desk lamp is in the seaside spirit. LEFT: A private garden outside the master bedroom creates an oasis. The pillow is embroidered with eyes of green glass beads that match the color of the client's exactly. ABOVE, LEFT: An array of Steuben aquatic sculptures. ABOVE, RIGHT: Her dressing room doors are inset with Fornasetti screens.

ABOVE AND RIGHT: To decorate a room with color this bold, simplify the palette. Vivid turquoise walls, curtains, and bedding details are balanced by a limited range of natural shades of wood and creamy hues of white. Decorative paint adds depth and softens the starkness of a solid bright color.

DAVID EASTON Timeless Elegance

Scavullo 50 Years

AMERICA'S PARKS

ABOVE AND RIGHT: The guest room scheme started with the hand-printed multicolored fabric on the headboard, with which the client fell in love. The traditional plaid design of the custom-colored rug is classic, but the large scale and funky colors feel modern. White linen curtains have an oversized blue cuff on the bottom and a small inset detail of green fabric.

LEFT: The four grandchildren, all boys, share a room decorated in a nautical theme of bunk beds, portholes, and fish-embroidered linens. ABOVE: On the connecting sleeping porch, the Boda Nova chandelier, porthole mirrors, and webbed chairs coexist with striped mattress ticking, the original pecky cypress ceiling, and plank wood floors.

FIFTH AVENUE FINESSE

THIS JEWEL BOX APARTMENT IS THE RESULT OF A renovation, which joined two apartments in a prestigious prewar Fifth Avenue apartment building.

The ambitious program for the 2,500 square-foot pied-à-terre called for a gracious main living space and small dining area, a discreet library, and three bedrooms. With the city's fine restaurants at hand, kitchen size was not a priority, and many constraints imposed by year-round daily living were dispensable. Designing this apartment was reminiscent of designing a yacht—and a most luxurious yacht at that!

With a relatively small footprint to design, details could be fully articulated and expressed in luxurious and intriguing ways. Using a classical vocabulary, the halls and baths (even the door frames) employ slab marble and onyx. The ceilings are articulated with complex plaster moldings, coffers, and vaults; walls are paneled, upholstered, or wrapped in leather. The subdued palette includes rich shades of cream, taupe, chocolate brown, and bronze.

The springboard behind the overall scheme was the clients' growing art collection, focusing on the twentieth-century, with an emphasis on Abstract Expressionism. An array of fine antiques was chosen to create a seamless overall look, resulting in a cohesive body of fine and decorative art that comes together as a collection of the highest caliber.

A long main hall benefits from interventions to help it appear more capacious, including dramatic art, a grid-patterned marble floor and vaulted ceiling that visually widen and lengthen the space, and a mirror at the far end.

ABOVE: In the entry vestibule, doorframes and floors are clad in marble to establish a feeling of great luxury. A subtly repeated diamond motif found in the gilded mounts of a neoclassical chest, the back splat of a black lacquer chair, and the marble design carved into the overhead doorframe unifies the decorative elements. The opulent range of materials continues deeper into the interior and includes furniture and accessories made of bronze, porphyry, lacquer, and ormolu in a calming palette of cream, taupe, and chocolate brown. RIGHT: A delicate garland on the mirror frame offsets the strict geometry of the diamond motif.

PREVIOUS PAGES: A symmetrical furniture plan and architectural elevation of paneled wood implies formality. Bronze details, including the fireplace surround and eighteenth-century tapestry fragments sewn onto throw pillows also make the room feel well dressed. ABOVE AND RIGHT: The attention to luxurious detail found throughout the apartment is epitomized in a pair of wood-framed klismos chairs upholstered in chocolate-dyed crocodile to emphasize their sculptural quality. Silk curtains are custom-stenciled and beaded. The quirky shape and inky ebony color of a grandfather clock make it a focal point of the living room—tall case clocks often function as wall sculpture by contrasting with two-dimensional works of art.

ABOVE: A custom bronze fireplace surround refers to the geometric motifs of the living room textiles and furniture and to the curtain hardware. RIGHT: Every detail in this apartment was carefully considered, down to lacquered placemats, designed to complement the fabrics and furniture. OVERLEAF: Closely related palettes unite the atmospheres of adjoining rooms and amplify available space. The apartment is designed with a minimum of circulation space, and the master bedroom opens directly onto the living room.

ABOVE, LEFT: An églomisé design connects mirrored closet doors thematically to the rest of the room, while also reflecting light back toward the bed against the opposite wall.
ABOVE, RIGHT AND RIGHT: The pattern in the bedroom is fully synchronized from the cornice design to the carpet, from the curtain trim to the headboard. An extra-wide frame allows the Joan Mitchell painting to fit proportionally in the space above the king-size bed.

ABOVE, RIGHT, AND OVERLEAF: In the library, a grid design comprised of large, lozenge-shaped and small, round nail heads adorns taupe-colored leather wall panels like jewelry. The repetition of the grid motif in the pillow trim and in the metal-framed side tables ties the room together, while the decorative inlay on the Japanese lacquer chest and the whorls of the python-skin lamps add a welcome curvilinear element.

HIGH STYLE IN A HIGH RISE

Raising four active children in an apartment in a busy city means that there will be few, if any, areas off-limits for visiting friends and family—no matter how big the apartment, it will never have a backyard or a basement to devote solely to recreation. Rather than fight against the inevitable takeover of every room, the owners of this apartment wisely chose a preemptive solution: to open up their entire home to all. They also, however, asked for a decorative solution that would still include elegant and calm spaces characterized by art, antiques, and other fine accessories.

Every room in this project multitasks whenever possible. Floor plans, for example, are designed to allow for large gatherings and small groups to be equally comfortable in every room, to accommodate a variety of activities. Combining the living and dining rooms to form one large entertainment area in the coveted corner of the apartment that reveals east and south views of the city skyline resulted in a casual feeling that the owners wanted. With large windows and uninterrupted flow, the public areas of the apartment now feel like a spacious loft.

Furniture was selected to be comfortable on a daily basis as well as appropriately formal for special occasions. Fabrics and finishes are durable and cleanable, but still elegant and customized. Lighting fixtures are abundant and stylish, take on a variety of forms—including ceiling lights, wall lights, and lamps—and are strategically placed to ensure that the mood can be modified depending on the gathering. The final design fuses traditional detailing, a modern shell, and a mix of furniture ranging from Regency to the 1940s through contemporary designs.

Subtly reflective finishes take advantage of the high floor and the daylight that filters in through unobstructed windows. A sideboard by Jules Leleu serves as a focal point in the living/dining room and also provides a generous amount of storage. Italian Art Deco patinated-bronze sconces on either side leave the surface open for buffet service or for art and objects when not in use. The light color and luster of the walls feels dressy; the surface is waxed to make it durable and wipeable. OVERLEAF: A Jean Arp sculpture, a ribbed vase, and a geometric pair of candlesticks make an intriguing arrangement of shape and materials on the coffee table. The lacquered wood and onyx top are protected by a gilt-bronze edge.

modern starts
PEOPLE PLACES THINGS

THE ABSTRACTION OF LANDSCAPE
FROM NORTHERN ROMANTICISM TO ABSTRACT EXPRESSIONISM

LELEU

JEAN-MICHEL FRANK

Hockney's People

CY TWOMBLY A MONOGRAPH

MO

ABOVE: The living room accessories speak to each other through their rounded forms, their translucence, and their amber-colored palette. RIGHT: Protective solar shades mounted above and behind the window frames can be easily lowered to prevent sun damage to the hand-embroidered silk curtain panels. Sheer flat panels at the top of the windows are decorative, staying slightly unfurled to soften the edge of the window frame.

Family rooms in cities do double duty by providing much-needed overflow space for play dates or for formal gatherings, and the design of this space focuses specifically on supporting dual functionality. Ottomans on casters slide under the coffee table for storage, but roll out to add extra seats to the room. Recessed ceiling lights around the perimeter of the room, a geometrically designed chandelier, and fluted crystal lamps provide several lighting options to create various moods, while blackout shades darken the room for movie matinees.

ABOVE AND RIGHT: The subtle repetition of a motif brings a welcome layer of harmony to any room design. Interlocking circles embroidered on a pillow and a similar geometric block print on curtain fabric draw the eye to a line of smooth nail heads on chair upholstery and to a table's shagreen veneer. Custom side tables flanking the sofa are particularly deep to provide storage for books and games and complement the palette of chocolate brown and ebonized wood.

PREVIOUS PAGES: The all-white kitchen design was driven by the client's desire for an entertaining space that felt large and open; a laser-cut marble backsplash adds a touch of drama. ABOVE: Brightly colored vases in rounded shapes help to temper the strong lines and crystalline white color of a kitchen's industrial materials. RIGHT: A custom light fixture's attenuated design creates a sculptural effect that echoes the rectangular forms of the dining table and the set of upholstered chairs.

A MIDCENTURY
MOUNTAIN RETREAT

A BROAD MOUNTAIN VISTA WAS THE POINT of departure for this project in Colorado, but the goal was not to resurrect cabin style or create a ski chalet. Instead, the interiors interpret rusticity through a modern prism. The architectural envelope is a sheath of dry-stacked stone, vintage wooden planks and timbers, and stone floors, all supplied by local artisans who transformed a newly built condominium into a vacation home replete with modern details and fine craftsmanship. The interior decoration is a hybrid of bold and refined elements, rough-hewn and smooth surfaces, contemporary furniture, and midcentury vintage pieces.

Enormous floor-to-ceiling windows that face the mountains, a river, and a cascade of trees run the entire length of one side of the apartment, but there are no windows on the opposite side, which left part of the interior in relative darkness. The solution was to cut a stairwell on the windowless side of the apartment, up two flights, to the top of the building, where skylights were added to let the sun in. This new vertical opening drops down through the duplex and tethers the apartment to the mountain by loosely evoking the feeling of a mineshaft.

Appropriately serene and suitable for all seasons, the apartment is now linked to the landscape and captures the feeling derived from arriving in a new place—and the intangible pleasure of being on vacation.

Walls are composed of alternating matte surfaces of striated and irregular stones and wood, creating a palette of natural shades of brown and gray, entirely without paint. An anodized-steel mantel shelf with exposed rivets contrasts with the rough surfaces of the wood and stone; its linear, man-made simplicity is juxtaposed with the natural surfaces surrounding it. Idiosyncratic decorations, like this Austrian horn sconce, one of a pair flanking the fireplace, are refined but not precious, and luxurious without being ostentatious.

ABOVE: A switchback staircase culminates in a skylight that floods the apartment with sunshine.
RIGHT: A strong horizontal rhythm established by stone floors, stone walls, and wooden planks is reinforced
in a custom carpet shaded in subtly varying tones of blue, green, and brown. The mount for a dramatic
bronze polar bear sculpture is integrated directly into the stacked wall stones. *Annie Oakley*, a lithograph by
Andy Warhol, a small early-twentieth-century Arts and Crafts butterfly table, and a contemporary
Austrian horn chair covered in baby lambskin are typical of the house's eclectic mix of decorative objects.

PREVIOUS PAGES: Furniture covered in chenille, fur, and suede complements the natural materials. Seating is arranged to allow guests to take advantage of the scenery outdoors as well as the conversation within; miniature club chairs tilt and swivel, and the nineteenth-century French tête-à-tête is placed parallel to the windows. LEFT: A farm implement with rolling wooden wheels makes a unique ottoman when fitted with a new leather top. The oversize weather vane is a focal point. ABOVE, LEFT: An angular, mid-twentieth-century side table fits well with the aesthetic of rectangles and squares anchored by a custom rug.
ABOVE, RIGHT: A table fitted with a tree trunk top relates thematically to the chairs surrounding it.

ABOVE: In the entryway, a rare Native American hide painted with scenes of a buffalo hunt hangs above an East Coast Adirondack bench. RIGHT: Sheets of anodized steel, which back the entry wall, also define a breakfast area. A Richard Prince photograph above the banquette and midcentury Swedish chairs demonstrate the success of pairing modern art and furniture with rustic elements.

MODERN TRADITIONAL

T HIS CLASSIC DUPLEX APARTMENT IS DESIGNED TO accommodate a busy young family's schedule and lots of social activity—school functions, board meetings, groups of children and teenagers. No rooms are off-limits, and there are no "touch-me-not" antiques. The decoration throughout relies on a confident mix of colorful modern art and on furniture treasured not for its age per se, but for its form and for the contribution each piece makes to the space as a whole.

In renovating the apartment, the owners sought to update systems and lighting within the original "bones" of the space—the stair carriage, room proportions, plasterwork, hardware, and so on. Now they have not only new air systems and custom closets, but also art lighting, a beautiful kitchen, elegant stone and wood floors, and even a new stair rail.

While generously proportioned this apartment felt dark because it's on a low floor with little natural light. This shadowy effect was especially evident in the entry foyer and was mitigated with an inlaid marble floor polished to reflect light. Interior doorways were enlarged to open up sight lines and create a more natural flow for circulation, and also to increase available light and views.

The eclectic furnishings are mostly late-eighteenth- and early-nineteenth-century antiques ranging from a Swedish neoclassical chest to a Biedermeier center table, as well as new pieces from contemporary designers. Bursts of colorful modern art—late-twentieth-century drawings and paintings and works by younger artists—animate the neutral envelope.

A cream-colored stone floor features a nautical star and a perimeter band of gray limestone and inset brass. The walls, finished in unwaxed gray stucco, contrast with the shiny texture of the floor. A richly burled wood table catches backpacks, letters, and newspapers. A tight, durable Scottish weave of blue and brown wool carpeting is tough as nails—even tougher than the nails of the apartment's resident cats. The curved wall above is hung with a nod to traditional salon style, which accommodates a variety of mediums and frames, and features works on paper by contemporary artists.

ABOVE: The disciplined elegance of an all-white painting and a tight cluster of bronze vessels is offset by a loose grouping of pink peonies and an irregularly shaped bronze sculpture painted in tones of sea-glass blue.
RIGHT: Antique carpets are often associated with color schemes of navy and orange when in fact they come in a wide range of hues; this one glows with bursts of denim blue and coral on a celadon green ground. Beige sofas, paper bag colored walls, white moldings, and a simple stone mantel create a tailored mood.

PREVIOUS PAGES: Warmth is created in a living room by an
infusion of colors, textures, and finishes. Curtains hang
full-length from just under the crown molding and break
gently on the floor to convey height. They are a similar
color to the walls, which gives the room a spacious feeling.
RIGHT: Brilliantly colorful artwork dictates the character
of a room; other furnishings should defer to it, not
compete with it. Classically shaped sofas and chairs, a
coffee table, antique end tables, and a pair of dark green
porcelain lamps with simple pulled-up linen shades are
all the additional embellishment this room requires.
An understated sofa is upholstered in beige linen velvet
and vintage chairs are covered in gray leather with a subtle
detail of oversized, spaced nail heads in a muted finish.

PREVIOUS PAGES, ABOVE, AND RIGHT: The palette of the dining room is built up in layers. A biscuit-colored rug, linen-colored walls, tobacco-colored curtains, and gold tones in the mirror and the lights contribute to the neutral but varied scheme. Orange tones, introduced here in the melon-colored chair seats, are warmly appetizing, universally flattering, and always successful in dining rooms. A linen white wall color is a restful foil to the intricate faux-ivory glaze on the ceiling. Circular ceiling molding calls for a round table below and contrasts with the square geometry of the room.

ABOVE: Rugs and wall treatments affect the moods of adjoining rooms as well as their own. In the library, a blue-and-brown Tabriz rug was chosen to support and defer to the palette and design of the adjacent living room rug and the stone entry floor. Walls are upholstered above the chair rail in natural, flax-colored linen to add variety to the wall treatments of the downstairs rooms without introducing another color. RIGHT: All of the art in the library is based around a humorous dessert theme.

ABOVE: Subway tiles refreshed with a miniature, stainless-steel treatment combine to form a shimmering kitchen backsplash that reflects natural light from the windows across the room. The countertops are black granite—possibly the most indestructible and forgiving material known— and the island is topped with Tundra Gray marble. Wooden floors add a warm contrast to the black, white, and silver theme, and feel comparatively soft underfoot. RIGHT: A cheerful breakfast nook gets some of the best daylight in the apartment. Blue-toned, softly constructed shades add a hint of curve. The work wheel is a reminder to enjoy the rituals of family life.

CELEBRATING AMERICANA

T
HIS CONNECTICUT HOUSE, SET AMID ACRES OF
wooded property threaded with riding paths, has been in the Cullman family for generations. Today its interiors reflect Ellie's personal taste and document her growth as a designer and collector.

Ellie's mantra has always been that no collection should be so revered, no house decorated around an aesthetic so rigorous, that you can't accommodate random or quirky objects you happen to love, and these interiors reflect that belief. Although a devoted collector of American antiques and folk art, she truly delights in blending disparate periods and styles. The house welcomes furnishings from every period and provenance: a pair of seventeenth-century Italian consoles, a pair of eighteenth-century French wind god weather vanes, a nineteenth-century English Aesthetic writing table, and twentieth-century garden ornaments. She includes anything that looks good with Americana, and it's all fun.

Heirloom furniture and ephemera—both precious and humble—mix easily with newer furnishings to give the rooms a warm informality that is accentuated by a cheerful palette. Patriotic reds and blues pop up in the dining room, but the overall palette is more vibrant and modern—with shades of creams, celadon, aquamarine, and coral.

The philosophy behind the house is rooted in a contemporary, almost Pop sensibility, where antiques are chosen for their strong graphic quality and bold color, where the installation is edited and fresh, creating strong connections and provocative parallels between the old and the new.

A bold, barn red, carved American eagle that once adorned a courthouse in Connecti-cut makes a strong introduction to Ellie's Americana collection. A grouping of game boards, humble and homemade, celebrates a confident use of color and abstraction typical of folk art, and also calls to mind the motifs and use of color found in modern art by Josef Albers, Jasper Johns, and Kenneth Noland. The pair of chairs, made for the American Centennial celebration, retain their original stars-and-stripes upholstery.

PREVIOUS PAGES AND RIGHT:
Balance between moments of
serene simplicity and a medley of
pattern and color defines the
living room. While the rug is
vividly patterned, for example,
the sofas are a cheerful but solid
beige chenille. The elaborately
embroidered raffia curtain cuffs
in a quilt pattern are tempered by
the main fabric, plain homespun
linen. Exuberant antiques and
accessories, ranging from
animal-shaped weather vanes to
folk art paintings, are set off by
walls simply painted a light
cream. At its core, the room
supports contemporary rituals of
family life with good and
plentiful lighting; low tables for
drinks, books, and games; and
ample, comfortable places to sit.

210 CULLMAN & KRAVIS

ABOVE: Objects from different countries and cultures mingle well with Americana. A boldly carved and brightly colored Napoleon III sideboard is entirely sympathetic with a display of folk art—both are characterized by painted surfaces and bold carving. RIGHT: A majestic eagle weather vane with a broad wingspan dominates a menagerie of animal forms in the living room.

LEFT: It's a good idea to leave the floors bare in a dining room, which may have to accommodate a variety of table configurations for family functions. With no rug, upholstered chairs add a good pop of color and pattern. Ellie's favorite object is the gold lion on top of the picture rail, one of a pair carved in 1911 that once adorned a synagogue in Philadelphia. ABOVE: A paired set of tables and mirrors flanking a fireplace benefits from slightly mismatched accessories to introduce variety, such as eighteenth-century chestnut bottles and antique rooster weather vanes.

LEFT: The entry hall sets a patriotic theme with a hooked rug commemorating the 1876 centennial and a tin-sheet weather vane painted as a flag. ABOVE: Grouping any substantial collection of similar objects creates an exciting dialogue between color and shape. Graniteware reminds Ellie of twentieth-century abstract artists such as Jackson Pollock with its swirly, playful patterning.

ABOVE: A mix of upholstered and wood-framed pieces is critical in decorating a room. "Personality chairs"—carved, painted, gilded, inlaid, embossed, and nail-studded— serve as foils for the large expanses of fabric on other seating. RIGHT: Animal imagery is one of the strongest themes of the collection, and appears here as a Tramp Art owl with amber-colored glass eyes and a pair of shore bird decoys.

Intensely colored and boldly inventive folk art and objects mix easily with new upholstery and a plainspoken sisal carpet to create a warm informality in the sunroom. The whimsical collection includes an antique bar sign, glove molds, oversize scissors, and a nearly life-sized wooden vintage milliner's statue. A palette of amber-toned wooden case pieces and honey-and-chalk-white upholstery defers to the greens and earth tones outside.

ABOVE AND RIGHT: In the sunroom, the ceiling and walls are paneled in beadboard, adding dimension and shadow. A grouping of nineteenth-century game boards, all carved and painted by hand, serve as art.

ABOVE: Game tables, frequently included in family rooms, provide a welcome surface for puzzles and games. Nineteenth-century hinges hung as artwork add intriguing forms and shadows to a wall—another example of how everyday objects can be elevated when used unexpectedly. RIGHT: The warmly aged tones of the iron elements, the wooden objects and furniture, and the muted tones of the soft furnishings all work together.

ABOVE: Paradoxically, a small room often feels bigger with saturated color on the walls. This tiny guest room neatly holds a nineteenth-century campaign bed found in Paris and "dressed" in fragments of vintage quilts. RIGHT: The back hall subtly repeats motifs found in the entry—stars, turned and painted furniture, and brightly colored textiles—and relates to the major space.

ABOVE AND RIGHT: Hand-embroidered, floral linen helps to delineate the shape of the master bedroom ceiling and give dimension to the space. The intricacy of the pattern calls for plain, white, raw silk curtains; a carpet featuring a large-scale plaid that does not compete with the wall fabric's repeat or design. This desk chair is upholstered with leather embossed in a corduroy texture.

Details, like a double row of faceted nail heads on a woven-linen headboard and crisp blue cuffs on pillow shams, add to the room's highly tailored sensibility. All of the lamps are white glass—some frosted, some opalescent—to add visual harmony to the space.

LEFT: The dressing room, open to the master bedroom, loosely adopts the larger room's decorative scheme. While the walls introduce the pattern in the bedroom, here the floral theme comes from the carpet. The dressing table is skirted in blue linen and embellished with brass, lozenge-shaped studs along the bottom hem for a couture touch. ABOVE: A large window seat becomes an unexpected, quiet reading nook.

VENETIAN VISION

WHEN A VACATION HOUSE BECOMES MORE OF A full-time residence, it tends to become a little more formal and it needs to be a little bit bigger. That's exactly what happened in this 1930s house on the Atlantic coast of Florida. An extensive renovation was undertaken to build a home that would be just the right size and have just the right feeling for the owners and their extended family.

The first step was to add a master suite and extra bedrooms and baths to accommodate the entire family. The next was to ensure that the interiors would relate well to the landscape and the ocean views. Floor-to-ceiling windows were designed for the principal rooms, and access to the outside from almost every room was confirmed in the new plans. Saturated shades of sunflower yellow, vermilion red, grass green and ocean blue were chosen to bring in the feeling of the sun, the water, and the plantings and, in particular, to evoke memories of trips to Italy, especially to Venice.

The rooms are spacious, bright, and cheerful, and there is a careful balance between a mix of reproductions, antiques, and treasured heirlooms. Italian materials—pietra dura, Venetian plaster, Murano glass—combine with furniture and paintings to create a warm Italian ambience.

Reflecting the sunny Florida location, a sunflower yellow palette saturates the living room. In a stroke of good luck, the owners' tric-trac table—a French table with a top that reverses from a game board to leather—is made of light fruitwood, which is well suited to these interiors, in contrast to more typical high-style mahogany and ormolu examples.

ABOVE: The focal point of the view corridor from the pool loggia is this Veneto-style garden well made of Vicenza stone. RIGHT: Raising the ceiling with a rectangular coffer mitigates the slightly narrow feeling of the living room. A hand-woven carpet in a Polonaise design was custom made for the space. Its large scroll pattern and its multicolored but tonal palette make the space appear wider. Antique wrought-iron sconces flank an eighteenth-century Venetian landscape painting. Jansen-style armchairs, covered in fanciful silk damask, and their gilt-wood carved bases echo the Italianate feeling.

The genesis for the living room design was the curtain fabric—a large-scale plaid silk taffeta—which boldly frames the long wall of windows facing the ocean view. A custom pair of gilt-wood chandeliers, each with serpentine arms and carved leaves, branches, and tassels, defines two separate seating areas. A pair of sofas, with tightly upholstered canted backs and swooping, sloped arms, opens up the room instead of dividing it in half, while gold-colored bullion trim sewn over the skirts adds an Old-World touch. The simple shape of the fireplace mantel allows the overscaled Venetian mirror and the antique candlesticks to stand out.

ABOVE, CLOCKWISE FROM TOP LEFT: French 1940s table with verde marble top; pillow embroidery inspired by an antique Italian textile; the pietra dura top of the coffee table is supported by a new custom metal base; the pillow embroidery enhances the Italianate look. RIGHT: The dining room walls are painted with a multicolored damask stencil overlaid with gold and copper to pull in all the colors of the furnishings. A slight offsetting of the stencil register creates shimmer and depth. Coquina floors keep the room from becoming too formal.

LEFT AND ABOVE: In the library, vermilion Venetian stucco walls support the groin-vaulted ceiling. A vintage tole-painted light fixture punctuates the stenciled ceiling. Sienna gold silk curtains with a blue cuff and an inset red flange, sky blue Roman shades, and a powder blue velvet chair and ottoman bring a strong geometric sensibility to the room. At the same time, the multicolored paisley sofa fabric and a coffee table with an inset wrought-iron grill and a crenelated edge add playful curves.

ABOVE: The dining loggia. RIGHT: The sunburst design on the back of the wicker chairs was inspired by a vintage Italian chair. A whitewashed oak table, a custom aquamarine and applegreen wool plaid rug, and a chandelier repainted to match the scheme add color and texture. A pass-through from the kitchen to the table makes family mealtimes easy.

LEFT: The master bedroom has a lovely feeling of transparency, conveyed by embroidered silk curtains and walls glazed in a liquid shade of blue. A gilt-wood chandelier and a bench upholstered in embossed suede with gold highlights subtly suggest the Italianate feeling of the rest of the house. Peacock blue silk velvet upholstered chairs add a bold accent. ABOVE: A periwinkle Murano chandelier matches the blue celeste stone of the bath deck. Shiny white Venetian stucco walls highlight the colored marble.

FRENCH FLAIR

BELOVED YEARLY VACATIONS IN THE FRENCH countryside led to the construction of this house in Connecticut, designed and decorated to recall those happy occasions. The owners have four children, four dogs, and a large extended family, so this house is truly lived in; every design decision fully reflects a feeling of commodious, welcoming, and stylish country living.

With plans and fabric swatches in hand, we made several shopping trips to Paris with the clients to source antique mantels, stone, wood flooring, light fixtures, and antiques. All were flown back to furnish the house: salvaged and period architectural elements are critical to the decoration of a newly constructed house such as this because they contribute a sense of age and remove the hard edges from modern materials to make a structure feel soft and beloved.

The family requested overscaled rooms, comfortable places to sit and read, game rooms, television rooms, a range of colors, and collections of unique objects. Luckily, the house is large enough to encompass many different activities and moods; however, an architectural and decorative framework is established to set up a rhythm and help tie the various spaces together. All main rooms, for example, have similarly beamed or coffered ceilings but different finish treatments. Additionally, the decorative details were carefully chosen and orchestrated to create a natural sense of flow from room to room. The house rambles pleasantly along as if it had been built up over decades rather than constructed all at once, benevolently embracing its energetic inhabitants and their activities. Its truly personal character and unique spirit results from the clients' allowing the objects they love to take center stage in their new home.

Several particularly French touches in the entry hall combine to create an immediately authentic mood. Paneled-oak front doors lead onto large, staggered bricks of polished French limestone, then to antique walnut parquet de Versailles in a satin finish that shows the luster of the darkly gleaming wood to advantage; walls painted in a trompe l'œil limestone texture recall the Bristol Hotel in Paris; and the oval-shaped entry stair is wrapped in a wrought-iron, wave-patterned rail inspired by Parisian ironwork. The five-foot-tall lantern was a lucky find at the Roland Garros flea market. Once its scratched glass panes were removed, it took on a somewhat modern, refreshed air, so they were not replaced and the frame was left open to bring a pleasant inside-outside, country feeling to the double-height space.

Reclaimed oak beams and a Louis XIV overmantel accentuate an eleven-foot-high ceiling in the living room, while coffers between the beams are discreetly distempered to look like aged plaster. The small-scale pattern and light celadon color of the chenille rug bring airiness and a relaxed feeling to the articulated millwork and the other detailed decorations. Three coffee tables anchor the seating arrangements, and their similarities ensure harmony, like variations on a theme. The round table in front of the fireplace features a specimen marble top with rich red and bronze tones; the table to its right has a red lacquer top and a gilt-bronze base; and the table by the windows has tiers of glass and bronze.

ABOVE, LEFT: Oversized and widely spaced nail heads highlight upholstery details on a yellow chenille sofa, and bands of ebony and bone inlay distinguish a side table. Both draw the eye and punctuate the pieces' unique forms. ABOVE, RIGHT: Tables that aren't brown or metal, round or square add welcome dimension to any room; this multicolored, painted-wood, octagonal-top table was a flea market find. RIGHT: Silk curtains with tassel fringe and sheer roman shades provide a respite from the grid of windows, while two Chinese ceremonial jade sculptures on stands speak to each other and add an unexpected Eastern touch. OVERLEAF: Wood-paneled coffers in the dining room are reflected in the diamond design of a sisal carpet below. Arches in the chair backs and in the windows are echoed in the arch seen in the Robert Polidori photograph, and marble obelisks flanking the doors to the terrace have topiary counterparts near the sideboard. All contribute to a subtle sense of harmony and proportion.

ABOVE: Uniquely charming curved corners, carved paws, and robust cabriole legs set at an atypical angle make a nineteenth-century console a signature piece. Above the chair rail, the wall is upholstered in celadon linen fabric with a tape detail along the edges; below, it is glazed and punctuated with nail heads that further reference the grids apparent on the ceiling and in the carpet. RIGHT: The curtain fabric has a lively edge of bellflowers on a woven tape binding and wooden tassels wrapped in silk.

ABOVE: Honey-colored veining in an antique French mantel made of Portoro marble was the inspiration for the study's warm golden tones. The custom white oak paneling was intentionally both rift- and quarter-sawn to reflect the look of many older houses, which naturally feature a variety of species, where any and all salvageable pieces would have been reused. This important detail helps to avoid the lack of character often associated with new woodwork. RIGHT: Homespun plaid wool carpet grounds the study and lends it a masculine note, while a collection of urns adds a historical reference.

The family room is at once open and cozy. In a single seating arrangement like this one with two large sofas, two upholstered arm chairs, and an oversize coffee table, one person can lie down, two or three can face the TV with their feet up, and those who want their own space can claim the big chairs. Gothic trusses and a wrought iron chandelier add drama, while large-scale photography in primary colors gives the room a contemporary feeling. A pair of hide-covered ottomans is a reminder that this is a working horse farm.

ABOVE: An iron armillary sphere and antique horse function as substantial tabletop sculptures that have enough presence and scale to draw attention even in a large and colorful room. As a tailored alternative to a tassel trim, the curtain cuff features a plaid wool fabric, a detail that also helps the oversized family room feel like a cozy den. RIGHT: Playing with fabrics on pillows is a fun way to add details without adding fuss. Solid fabrics can be rendered in a diamond design, or a striped fabric sewn to make a boxlike motif that references shapes found elsewhere in a room.

Beyond the Dunes
A Portrait of the

The American Townhouse
BY KEVIN J. MURPHY PHOTOGRAPHS BY RADEK KURZAJ

STABLES   Majestic Spaces for Hor

The Gardens of Russell Page

FLORA'S ORCHIDS

ABOVE: The kitchen, with its ornately carved stone, wood, and wrought-iron hardware, epitomizes French country style. A tile backsplash featuring topiaries and verdure conveys a garden feeling. RIGHT: Blending functionality and style, woven resin bistro chairs add color, are simple to clean, and easy to move around, which is nice when dogs and kids are underfoot. Swag-and-jabot window dressings stay away from potential messes and crumbs, and are an ideal way to finish a curved bay window. Café curtains add privacy and mitigate nighttime reflections that can turn low panes into inhospitable black mirrors.

ABOVE AND RIGHT: On one side of an octagonal sunroom, a mantel fashioned from rough French limestone, an exposed brick wall, and terracotta lions bring the outdoors in. The architectural vocabulary from the other main rooms is translated here into beams, vaults, pilasters, and boarding painted a milky white to reflect country light. Accents of grass green and burnt sienna in fabrics and basket-colored wicker furniture harmonize into a warm, welcoming palette that feels right for the country.

266 CULLMAN & KRAVIS

ABOVE AND RIGHT: One color—cornflower blue—unites fabrics of
different scales in the master bedroom. A small-scale trellis pattern on
the carpet, large-scale plaid on the curtains, and toile on the walls and
upholstery cocoon the room in the single, soothing hue. Leather-
wrapped side tables mingle with the rich wood tones of an antique side
chair, round table, and chandelier, and also provide closed and
open storage and a surface for reading lamps—at just the right height.

CREDITS

FRENCH FORTIES ON THE PARK
PROJECT MANAGERS: Melissa Koch, Elena Phillips
ARCHITECT: John B. Murray Architect
CONTRACTOR: Peter Cosola Inc.
PHOTOGRAPHY: Eric Piasecki

GEORGIAN ELEGANCE
PROJECT MANAGERS: Jenny Fischbach, Lizzy Dexter
ARCHITECT: Allan Greenberg Architect
CONTRACTOR: Xhema
LANDSCAPE DESIGNER: Deborah Nevins & Associates, Inc.
ART CONSULTANT: Thea Westreich Art Advisory Services
PHOTOGRAPHY: Eric Piasecki

UP COUNTRY MAUI
PROJECT MANAGERS: Lizzy Dexter, Allison Davis, Cristin deVeer, and Lynn Hancock
ARCHITECT OF RECORD: John B. Murray Architect
DESIGN ARCHITECT: Jeff Wooley Architect
CONTRACTOR: TMC Contracting
LANDSCAPE DESIGNER: Hunton Conrad & Associates
PHOTOGRAPHY: Eric Piasecki

LUMINOUS LUXURY
PROJECT MANAGERS: Alyssa Urban, Katie Sutton
ARCHITECT: Allan Greenberg Architect
CONTRACTOR: Xhema
ART CONSULTANT: Thea Westreich Art Advisory Services
PHOTOGRAPHY: Eric Piasecki

RUSTIC REDUX
PROJECT MANAGERS: Claire Ratliff, Isabel Rutherfoord
ARCHITECT: Resort Design Associates/ Gordon Pierce
CONTRACTOR: George Shaeffer Construction
PHOTOGRAPHY: David Marlow

ASIAN FUSION
PROJECT MANAGERS: Lizzy Dexter, Allison Davis
ARCHITECT: John B. Murray Architect
CONTRACTOR: Interior Management
PHOTOGRAPHY: Eric Piasecki

PALM BEACH PUNCH
PROJECT MANAGERS: Claire Ratliff, Sarah DePalo
ARCHITECT: Thomas M. Kirchhoff Architects
CONTRACTOR: Worth Builders
LANDSCAPE ARCHITECT: Niviera Williams Design
ART CONSULTANTS: Graham & Friedrich
PHOTOGRAPHY: Eric Piasecki

FIFTH AVENUE FINESSE
PROJECT MANAGERS: Alyssa Urban, Sarah DePalo
ARCHITECT: John B. Murray Architect
CONTRACTOR: Peter Cosola Inc.
ART CONSULTANT: Thea Westreich, Art Advisory Services
PHOTOGRAPHY: Durston Saylor; Tom McWilliam pages 151, 154, 160, 161, 162

HIGH STYLE IN A HIGH RISE
PROJECT MANAGERS: Jenny Fischbach, Allison Davis
ARCHITECT: Andrew Pollock
CONTRACTOR: Zale Contracting, Inc.
ART CONSULTANT: Rachel Carr Goulding
PHOTOGRAPHY: Durston Saylor

A MIDCENTURY MOUNTAIN RETREAT
PROJECT MANAGERS: Claire Ratliff, Isabel Rutherfoord
ARCHITECT: Mosaic Architects/Jane Snyder
CONTRACTOR: George Shaeffer Construction
PHOTOGRAPHY: David Marlow

MODERN TRADITIONAL
PROJECT MANAGERS: Tracey Pruzan, Allison Davis
ARCHITECT: John B. Murray Architect
CONTRACTOR: Peter Cosola Inc.
PHOTOGRAPHY: Eric Piasecki

CELEBRATING AMERICANA
PROJECT MANAGERS: Lee Cavanaugh, Cristin deVeer
ARCHITECT: John B. Murray Architect
CONTRACTOR: Bacco, Inc.
PHOTOGRAPHY: Eric Piasecki

VENETIAN VISION
PROJECT MANAGERS: Alyssa Urban, Katie Sutton
ARCHITECT: Jeffrey Smith
CONTRACTOR: Sands Construction
LANDSCAPE ARCHITECT: Innocenti & Webel
PHOTOGRAPHY: Eric Piasecki

FRENCH FLAIR
PROJECT MANAGER: Lee Cavanaugh
ARCHITECT: Elliot Rosenblum, Jason Hwang, Izumi Shepard
CONTRACTOR: Taconic Builders
LANDSCAPE ARCHITECT: Wesley Stout
ART CONSULTANT: Lorinda Ash
PHOTOGRAPHY: Eric Piasecki

Page 2
PROJECT MANAGERS: Lee Cavanaugh, Tracey Pruzan, Alyssa Urban, Katie Sutton
ART CONSULTANT: Rachel Carr Goulding
PHOTOGRAPHY: Nick Johnson

Page 4
PROJECT MANAGER: Jenny Fischbach
ARCHITECT: Timothy Greer
CONTRACTOR: Zale Contracting Inc.
ART CONSULTANT: Rachel Carr Goulding
PHOTOGRAPHY: Durston Saylor

Page 6
PROJECT MANAGER: Lee Cavanaugh
ARCHITECT: John B. Murray Architect
CONTRACTOR: Cornerstone Builders
LANDSCAPE ARCHITECT: Martha Baker
PHOTOGRAPHY: Tom McWilliam

ACKNOWLEDGMENTS

I love decorating and design, and I am beyond grateful to all of the people whose efforts allow me to pursue my passion every day. I owe special thanks to Tracey Pruzan, my colleague and cohort for almost twenty years. Tracey has been my most valued and creative partner on this book, capturing the essence of our work with her eloquent words.

Of course, none of this would be possible without our clients, who have been a constant inspiration, always taking us to new places, both literally and figuratively. Thank you for trusting Cullman & Kravis to realize your vision.

My endless gratitude extends, of course, to my amazing design partners present—Lee Cavanaugh, Claire Ratliff, and Alyssa Urban; and partners past—Lizzy Dexter and Jenny Fischbach. Special thanks to our current invaluable staff: Amanda Darnell, Allison Davis, Sarah DePalo, Alison Eddy, Ali Epstein, Lynn Hancock, Melissa Koch, Lindsay Saccullo, Katie Sutton, Andrea Ashe Tutt, and Caroline White, and, able designers each, who not only keep the projects running smoothly but also the office fully stocked with cupcakes and iced coffee. I will always be extremely grateful to Ellen Chopay, our financial controller and office manager, and to Joe Cavaliere, who gets us and our "stuff" from A to B.

This book could not have become a reality without Gianfranco Monacelli, who wanted to show our work "up close." We are forever grateful for the wisdom of Stacee Lawrence and Elizabeth White, our smart and savvy editors. I am enormously indebted to our dynamic book agent, Jill Cohen, who skillfully guided us through this entire process, and to our brilliant book designer, Doug Turshen, who created the magnificent layouts that grace these pages. Steve Turner's computer wizardry was also a key component, presenting the magical photographs of Nick Johnson, David Marlow, Tom McWilliam, Durston Saylor, and especially Eric Piasecki.

Thanks also to the architects and contractors whose talent and expertise are evident here. Wow! To our many vendors—especially Beauvais, Anthony Lawrence Belfair, E. Braun, M. Gabaree, Holland & Sherry, Lamptouch, Larrea, Lesage, Lowy, Paul Maybaum, Penn & Fletcher, Pintura, Platypus, Ranjit Ahuja, Eli Rios, Sterling, Allen Thorp, Urban-Delta, Mark Uriu, Gabe Velazquez, Andrew Webb, Steve Williams, and to all the people in the D&D building who give us samples, answer our questions and help us meet deadlines—you make every day in our business not just possible but also rewarding and worthwhile.

Very special thanks to Paige Rense, Margaret Russell, and all of the exceptional editors, writers, and bloggers who have recognized and supported our work over the years. I must also thank our publicist Christina Juarez for her enthusiasm and ideas.

Every business is a village, and ours wouldn't be complete without MZ Movers, MTS messenger service, and the delivery people from Burger Heaven. The list goes on and on!

To my husband, Edgar, who has optimistically survived my never-ending decorating projects at home; to my children—Trip, Sam, and Georgina—who have generously volunteered their unsolicited critiques over the years, and to the amazing Ana, who keeps me healthy, organized, and always on time!

This book is dedicated to my late partner Hedi, with whom I shared the courage and the vision to start this business almost thirty years ago. I think about you every day.

Published in the United States by The Monacelli Press

Library of Congress Control Number 2013935944

ISBN 9781580933551

10 9 8 7 6 5 4 3 2 1

First edition

Designed by Doug Turshen with Steve Turner

Printed in China

www.monacellipress.com